THE OFFICIAL
HEART OF MIDLOTHIAN
ANNUAL 2020

Written by Andrew Petrie
Designed by Paul Galbraith and John Anderson

A Grange Publication

© 2019. Published by Grange Communications Ltd., Edinburgh, under licence from Heart of Midlothian. Printed in the EU.

Photographs © SNS Group
ISBN 978-1-913034-20-7

CONTENTS

Welcome

Hello and welcome to The Official Heart of Midlothian football Club Annual 2020.

Within the pages of this year's annual, you can read all about the 2018/19 season, our aims for the season ahead, and all about the Women's Team which has officially become a part of the club.

Last year was a strange one for the team as we had two fantastic cup runs and sat at the top of the table in November, but ultimately finished sixth in the league. Our performance in the Scottish Cup was a highlight and leading the boys out at Hampden was not just one of the best moments of my career, but one of the best of my life. Unfortunately, it wasn't meant to be but hopefully we made the fans proud.

We also recorded a fantastic win at Easter Road (thanks Olly), and yet again beat Celtic at Tynecastle Park at the start of the season. We played our first full season in front of the new Main Stand and we hope to keep filling it to capacity in 2020.

We welcomed a few new faces to Tynecastle Park this summer – and a few familiar ones! It was great to add Naisy to the dressing room permanently, alongside Glenn Whelan who adds even more experience than me! I've also been joined in defence by Craig Halkett – although he's been scoring like a striker!

It is great to have Jamie Walker back home, alongside another quality attacking option in Conor Washington. We've also brought in Premier League quality with Joel Pereira and Loïc Damour and I'm sure this is the strongest squad we have had in years.

In the dressing room, we know that the team didn't meet our expectation in the league. However, the early season form showed what we are truly capable of and I can assure you we will do our utmost to bring that form back to Tynecastle Park.

Walking out at Hampden Park in May, surrounded by over 20,000 Hearts fans, just reminded me of how lucky I am to captain this great club. The armband is a responsibility I wear with great pride and, after signing my new contract last season, it's an honour I hope I can hold until the end of my playing career.

As always - Hearts, Hearts, Glorious Hearts!

Christophe Berra

(Captain)

7

FIVE of the BIGGEST

2018/19 WAS ANOTHER ROLLERCOASTER SEASON FOR THE JAMBOS.

After 11 league games Craig Levein's side were flying high at the top of the table, but serious injuries to many key players brought them back down to earth. Despite the losses of Christophe Berra, John Souttar, Uche Ikpeazu, Steven Naismith, Peter Haring and Michael Smith at various points of the season, the boys were able to reach the League Cup semi-final and the Scottish Cup Final – the first time that double feat has been achieved in 14 years.

EVERYONE IN!
The boys celebrate together after Kyle Lafferty's match-winning volley.

SWEET AS A NUT
Kyle Lafferty's 56th minute volley was hit perfectly, finding the bottom corner to give Craig Gordon no chance.

IT'S A GOOD LAUGH, ISN'T IT
Steven Naismith... shares a laugh... with Jack Hendry after a free-kick decision.

HEARTS 1 - 0 CELTIC

DATE:	11th August 2018
LOCATION:	Tynecastle Park

GET IN!
Uche and Kyle Lafferty give an impromptu piggyback to Steven Naismith as they celebrate the winning goal!

UCHPOWER
Jozo Simunovic and Scott Brown soon find out that you can't simply win the ball back off Uche Ikpeazu.

CLEAN SHEET
Bobby Zlamal picks up the first of eight clean sheets he would keep in his debut season at Tynecastle.

9

HEARTS 4 - 2 MOTHERWELL

| DATE: | 26th September 2018 |
| LOCATION: | Tynecastle Park |

KABOOM
Steven Naismith whips out his new trademark celebration after scoring the goal that secured passage to the semi-final.

C'MERE YOU
Steven MacLean and John Souttar get a little bit too close as they defend a corner.

UNBE-LEE-VABLE
Olly Lee celebrates as Hearts fend off Motherwell's comeback to regain the lead.

YOUNG GUN

Callumn Morrison continued to impress after breaking into the first team at the start of the season.

MAC-ATTACK

Steven MacLean showed his predatory instinct to put Hearts ahead in the first-half.

11

HIBS 0 - 1 HEARTS

DATE:	29th December 2018
LOCATION:	Tynecastle Park

READY, AIM, FIRE
Olly Lee takes aim as he prepares to blast a rocket towards goal.

OLLY, OLLY LEE
The Englishman can hardly believe it as he scores one of the finest goals in Derby history.

DOYLE TO THE RESCUE
Colin Doyle gets his fingertips to Steven Whittaker's goal-bound effort, brushing it onto the post before it spins across the goal line and out!

ANGEL EYES

Find someone who looks at you the way Ben Garuccio looks at Olly Lee.

THE SKIPPER'S ROAR

Christophe Berra can be heard around the city as he joins the fans in celebrating a famous win.

SALUTE

The Jambo Soldier, Clevid Dikamona, salutes the fans after he battled through injury to complete the game.

HEARTS 3 - 0 INVERNESS

DATE:	13th April 2019
LOCATION:	Hampden Park

WHO'S SCORED?!
John Souttar gets on the scoresheet for only the second time in his Hearts career.

H.H.G.H.
The boys celebrate together in front of the maroon faithful.

YYYYAAAAASSSSS
Bobby Burns roars with joy after the second goal.

GAME, SET AND MATCH

Sean Clare's goal ends the game as a contest as the Jambos take an unassailable lead.

BROTHERS IN ARMS

Centre-back duo Christophe Berra and John Souttar celebrate together at full-time.

"I TOLD YOU I'D SCORE, GAFFER"

Uche Ikpeazu and Craig Levein embrace after the Englishman's opening goal.

HEARTS 1 - 2 CELTIC

DATE:	25th May 2019
LOCATION:	Hampden Park

HUG ME, BROTHER
Ryan Edwards is mobbed by his teammates, Michael Smith, Sean Clare and Steven MacLean after scoring the opener.

REMEMBER THE NAME
16-year-old Aaron Hickey started the Scottish Cup Final, keeping POTY James Forrest quiet for the entire 90 minutes. He was just nine when Hearts beat Hibs 5-1 in 2012.

NUTS
Ryan Edwards puts the Jambos 1-0 up with a cool close-range finish.

IF YOU CANNAE SPELL IT THEN HERE'S WHAT IT SAYS

Ryan Edwards started March 2019 in the reserve squad, without a first team appearance to his name. He got his head down and worked hard and ended up starting and scoring in a Scottish Cup Final.

HEARTS HERO

Ryan Edwards celebrates putting Hearts ahead.

CHEESE

Hearts battled on May 25th but it was not meant to be. The boys did themselves proud and it won't be the last time they play at Hampden.

A HISTORY OF

HEART OF MIDLOTHIAN WOMEN FC (HMWFC) HAS OPERATED INDEPENDENTLY SINCE ITS PARTNERSHIP WITH HEART OF MIDLOTHIAN FC IN 2009. SINCE THEN, HMWFC HAS GROWN INTO A HIGH-ACHIEVING COMMUNITY CLUB WITH A FULL PATHWAY FROM UNDER-9S TO SENIOR LEVEL.

Many of these teams have won Scottish League Cup titles and played in national performance leagues, in addition to the first team who have competed regularly in the Scottish Women's Premier League 2.

For the last 10 years, HMWFC have been run by highly-motivated volunteers and coaches, driven to provide the best footballing opportunities for women and girls who want to play the game under the Hearts name.

In their success over the last few years, HMWFC developed a strong aspiration to compete at the highest level possible and become an elite performance club. With the Men's Academy in a strong position, the decision to integrate women and girl's football into the Academy turned into an organisational priority.

The joint vision to advance women and girls' football at Hearts allowed HMWFC and HMFC to devise a plan for transition and full integration come November 2019.

▲ Midfield Dynamo: Rachel Walkingshaw

HEARTS WOMEN *so far...*

We look back at the last ten years with gratitude and awe for the many volunteers who have dedicated their time and commitment to women and girls' football under the Hearts name.

The journey we embark on now has been paved by their hard work. We look ahead to an exciting new season with women and girls' football fully integrated into HMFC.

We are one club, one passion, one Hearts.

BIG NEWS & FUTURE PLANS

It is a huge time of change in women's football, with things slowly heading in the right direction. The summer of 2019 will go down in history for the sport and at Hearts, it was no different. They were preparing for the opening of the women's side of the Academy, which was to become fully integrated into the club in November.

The announcement was made in December 2018, when Chairman Ann Budge announced that the club was pouring a six-figure annual investment into the women's side and academy. Manchester City Women's technical director Kevin Murphy - a Hearts fan himself - was coming to the club to build the

Mutch Ado About Nothing: Emily Mutch

■ Laying Down the Law: Mariel Kaney
▼ Super Striker: Lauren Evans

Everybody In!

19

A HISTORY OF HEARTS WOMEN
so far...

Academy from the ground up. In the summer of 2019, Hearts sat top of the table in the SPWL 2 - the second division in Scottish women's football. The Jambos have never been in the top flight, but it looks like that is about to change.

Promotion to the top flight is the ambition for the side, who have seen the arrival of numerous new players as they gear up to try and become one of the biggest forces in Scottish football.

Striker Mariel Kaney has been with the club since the summer of 2018 and balances her football career with her job as a solicitor. She spoke to HeartsTV in June, just ahead of the 2019 World Cup, and told us how much she is looking forward to the future.

"I think it's an amazing thing to see and it's quite an interesting time to be at the club," Mariel said. "Hearts are definitely one of the frontrunners and people are looking at the club thinking Hearts are going to be the ones to pull through in the next few years.

"With that comes a bit of pressure, but also a lot of excitement because there's opportunities that other teams and other girls aren't getting. It's something that, as players, we've been pushing

for, for a long, long time quietly. Quietly fighting a battle that nobody's seeing.

"Now, you can see all the media attention Scotland are getting with the World Cup. The game is changing so it's amazing to be a part of it, and Hearts are going to lead the way."

Midfielder Jennifer Smith grew up supporting the club and admitted herself that she never could have imagined playing for Hearts when she grew up. In May 2019 she got the chance to play at Tynecastle when the Jambos hosted Dundee United in Gorgie, instead of their usual home at the Oriam.

"No, I wouldn't have expected it to be honest," she laughed. "To be able to play at Tynecastle was a big thing as well, to be able to play where the men play and have that opportunity, it was great.

"I was very nervous before, when we were training at the start a lot of people were coming in and I didn't expect so many people to come, but it was just the best experience."

Jennifer, alongside teammate Emily Mutch, was called up to the Scotland Under-19s squad for the European Championships over the summer.

"I find it very challenging because I go away with the Scotland Under-19s as well. It's hard to balance out school and be away at the same time, but we get the opportunity when we're there but have to catch up when we get back.'

Jennifer is one of a number of young players who have broken through into the first team in the last few months, with fellow Hearts fan Claire Delworth starting most games at right-back.

"It's been such an inspiration because women's football has grown so much bigger than what it used to be," Jennifer said. "For me, I've been inspired to be in that team, so it's definitely given me a goal to be in there."

Captain Fantastic: Danni Pagliarulo

Aisha Maughan

(L-R) Teenage kicks: Jennifer Smith, Emily Mutch and Claire Delworth

HEARTS WOMEN MANAGER:
Kevin Murphy

In January 2019, Hearts were delighted to announce the arrival of Kevin Murphy. He joined us from Manchester City and he's been appointed the Hearts Girls Academy and Women's Manager. We sat down with him for a little Q&A to get to know more about him and his plans for the future.

Firstly Kevin, tell us a little bit about yourself! We understand you're also Hearts fan...
Well, I am currently the Hearts Girls Academy and Women's Manager, having been Technical Director at Manchester City and Rangers previously for their women's sections. Yes, it's true, I am a Jambo! Despite being from Hamilton, I grew up as a Hearts fan. My cousin played for Hearts at the time and being a young kid, I wanted to support him. That led to me being a Hearts fan - although I didn't get to as many games as I would have liked!

How did you originally get into women's football?
I got into women's football through my partner, Lynsey. She used to watch me play for my local team on a Saturday and I would go watch her play for Hamilton Accies on a Sunday. I was asked to step in and help assist whilst they were looking for new coaches - little did I know I would end up there for nine seasons.

What first attracted you to leaving Manchester City and joining Hearts?
Being a Hearts fan was a huge draw, as was the opportunity to come back home to Scotland where all my family are based. However, when Roger Arnott - the Head of Academy - sat with me and discussed the club's plan for girls and women's football, I was instantly hooked. I firmly believe we are doing big things for women's football in Scotland and to be part of the journey from the start was a real attraction. I was pulled by the project, the ambition and the drive the club has to make it happen. I wanted to be part of that.

Where would you like the Hearts Women's side to be in five years' time?
In five years' time, I would hope the team are in the top league, competing for silverware and Champions League football. The club, although relatively new, have never won a major trophy domestically or represented Scotland in the Champions League so those are burning ambitions I have. I also want to oversee the Girls Academy which will operate in the exact same fashion as it does with the Boys. I hope this will encourage more talented girls to an elite environment so they can reach their full potential. I would love to see Hearts girls and women's players represent Scotland nationally, across all age groups.

For any young girls reading, what does this news mean for them and why should they choose Hearts if they want to get into football?
It doesn't matter if you are a boy or a girl - you can dream of playing for Hearts. Now, girls can dream of wearing the famous maroon whilst in an elite training environment at our Academy. We will offer equal opportunities to all girls, at the same level as the boys receive - which doesn't happen at many clubs. Not only at the elite level do we offer opportunities, but the community department are doing more for girls-only activities as well, so no matter the level of experience/ability, you can play for Hearts.

We've got some fantastic young players in the squad already - Jennifer Smith, Claire Delworth and Emily Mutch to name a few! How big a part can they play, and what are your hopes for them?
Hopefully they can play a huge part in the future. We want to develop well rounded players who are good people, too. Those who you mentioned are talented players with lots of potential and we would hope we can add to that talent and further enhance the squad to compete at the highest level. Keeping our best young players are integral to that.

SPOT THE BALL

CAN YOU SPOT WHICH IS THE REAL BALL IN THE BELOW PHOTOS?

Answers on page 60-61.

JAMBO WORDSEARCH

FIND THE HEARTS WORDS IN THE GRID.
WORDS CAN GO HORIZONTALLY, VERTICALLY AND DIAGONALLY IN ALL EIGHT DIRECTIONS.

D	L	E	I	F	T	A	E	H	W	H
N	D	N	R	Z	L	H	H	K	R	D
F	A	E	R	K	H	D	L	E	O	T
R	Y	I	Y	U	M	T	K	Y	Y	D
K	C	G	S	M	B	L	L	E	C	E
K	C	R	R	M	A	E	K	N	K	L
Y	E	O	K	W	I	C	S	C	M	W
K	H	G	J	M	I	T	M	O	Q	O
V	C	R	K	H	P	H	H	M	R	R
F	U	J	S	K	A	C	E	L	B	T
W	H	A	L	K	E	T	T	R	M	H

DELWORTH	HICKEY	SKACEL
DOYLE	JOCK	UCHE
GORGIE	NAISMITH	WALKER
HALKETT	ROSEBURN	WHEATFIELD

Answers on page 60-61.

PLAYER

NAME
Zdenek Zlamal
POSITION
Goalkeeper
NATIONALITY
Czech Republic
DoB
05/11/85

NAME
Colin Doyle
POSITION
Goalkeeper
NATIONALITY
Rep. of Ireland
DoB
12/06/85

NAME
Joel Pereira
POSITION
Goalkeeper
NATIONALITY
Portugal
DoB
28/06/96

NAME
Michael Smith
POSITION
Defender
NATIONALITY
Northern Ireland
DoB
04/09/88

NAME
Jamie Brandon

POSITION
Defender

NATIONALITY
Scotland

DoB
05/02/98

NAME
Christophe Berra

POSITION
Defender

NATIONALITY
Scotland

DoB
31/01/85

NAME
John Souttar

POSITION
Defender

NATIONALITY
Scotland

DoB
25/09/96

NAME
Aaron Hickey

POSITION
Defender

NATIONALITY
Scotland

DoB
10/06/02

NAME
Craig Halkett

POSITION
Defender

NATIONALITY
Scotland

DoB
29/05/95

NAME
Clevid Dikamona

POSITION
Defender

NATIONALITY
Rep. of Congo

DoB
23/06/90

NAME
Aidy White

POSITION
Defender

NATIONALITY
Rep. of Ireland

DoB
10/10/91

NAME
Ben Garuccio

POSITION
Defender

NATIONALITY
France

DoB
15/06/95

NAME
Bobby Burns

POSITION
Defender

NATIONALITY
Northern Ireland

DoB
07/10/99

NAME
Loïc Damour

POSITION
Midfielder

NATIONALITY
French

DoB
08/01/91

NAME
Callumn Morrison

POSITION
Midfielder

NATIONALITY
Scotland

DoB
05/07/99

NAME
Jake Mulraney

POSITION
Midfielder

NATIONALITY
Rep. of Ireland

DoB
05/04/96

NAME
Anthony McDonald

POSITION
Midfielder

NATIONALITY
Scotland

DoB
17/03/01

NAME
Oliver Bozanic

POSITION
Midfielder

NATIONALITY
Australia

DoB
08/01/89

NAME
Connor Smith

POSITION
Midfielder

NATIONALITY
Scotland

DoB
01/02/02

NAME
Peter Haring

POSITION
Midfielder

NATIONALITY
Austria

DoB
02/06/93

PLAYER PROFILES

NAME
Harry Cochrane

POSITION
Midfielder

NATIONALITY
Scotland

DoB
24/04/01

NAME
Andy Irving

POSITION
Midfielder

NATIONALITY
Scotland

DoB
13/05/00

NAME
Glenn Whelan

POSITION
Midfielder

NATIONALITY
Rep. of Ireland

DoB
13/01/84

NAME
Sean Clare

POSITION
Midfielder

NATIONALITY
England

DoB
18/09/96

NAME
Jamie Walker

POSITION
Midfielder

NATIONALITY
Scotland

DoB
25/06/93

NAME
Aidan Keena

POSITION
Striker

NATIONALITY
Rep. of Ireland

DoB
25/04/99

NAME
Steven MacLean
POSITION
Striker
NATIONALITY
Scotland
DoB
23/08/82

NAME
Steven Naismith
POSITION
Striker
NATIONALITY
Scotland
DoB
14/09/86

NAME
Uche Ikpeazu
POSITION
Striker
NATIONALITY
England
DoB
28/02/95

NAME
Conor Washington
POSITION
Striker
NATIONALITY
Northern Ireland
DoB
18/06/92

NAME
Craig Wighton
POSITION
Striker
NATIONALITY
Scotland
DoB
27/07/97

NAME
Ryotaro Meshino
POSITION
Striker
NATIONALITY
Japanese
DoB
18/06/98

Hearts Academy

HEART OF MIDLOTHIAN HAS HAD A LONG HISTORY OF BRINGING PLAYERS THROUGH THEIR YOUTH SQUADS AND INTO THE FIRST TEAM. IN 2020, THIS TREND IS SET TO CONTINUE.

Since its opening in 2004, the Academy has seen hundreds of players pass through its doors with some going on to play internationally and others going on to thrive in different careers entirely.

Obviously, the coaches and backroom staff at The Oriam are desperate to see the young lads they've coached grow as footballers and end up playing on the Tynecastle turf. For a number of them, that dream has become a reality - with 24 players going on to play more than 38 games - a whole season - for the first team.

In recent years, the man spearheading that charge has been Roger Arnott, manager of the Academy. He took up the post in 2014, when the club was enduring its darkest spell. However, thanks to his help - along with first team manager and Director of Football Craig Levein - the mini Jambos coming through the Academy have helped the club survive and thrive.

Roger, how confident are you that the Academy youngsters can make an impact on the first team in 2020?
It is very difficult to predict how the young Academy graduates will adapt to their new surroundings of life in professional football. The demands of the players physically and mentally are much tougher than within the Academy - they have to cope with the relentless strain on their bodies on a daily basis and at a higher intensity than they are previously used to. The key to each individual player's development is for our coaching and support staff to recognise that they all develop and mature at different rates, and not to expect them all to progress at the same degree in their first season. So, whilst I am always

confident about the ability of our young players, we must recognise that patience is key.

How far can the current crop of youngsters - Harry Cochrane, Connor Smith, Aaron Hickey, Anthony McDonald and Andy Irving - go?
All of these players have been involved with the Scotland national youth teams at some stage or another and have demonstrated in that arena that they can compete with some of the best young players and nations in Europe. I believe that all of those players - and others within the club - are only at the beginning of a very long and successful career in football and if they continue to work hard and apply themselves on a daily basis, then they will continue to improve. I am certain that, if they want it badly enough, they can go on to play for some of the best clubs in Europe and help to shape the Scotland national team in the future.

What do you, as head of the Academy, look for in a young player?
Firstly, young players must have a hunger and desire to play football, regardless of their age. Those young players who absolutely love playing and training and who enjoy working hard to

improve every session are the types of players we want to see at the club. Aside from that, we look at their physicality, their technical ability and knowledge of the game. But most of these aspects can be worked on by the Academy staff. If we have someone with a good base level and great desire and enthusiasm, then we will work hard to make them better players.

Why should young players pick Hearts as the team to play for?

This is the most crucial decision a parent and young player can make at, sometimes, a very young age but this has to be based on three things:
1. Does the club have a pathway and a history of progressing young players?
2. Does the club develop players capable of playing at the top level?
3. Is the environment right for developing young players?

Our track record shows that we have a history of progressing young players, many of whom have reached the top level. We believe the club has the best technical development programme for young players in the world, with Box Soccer, led by ex-Hearts Under-20s coach, Darren Murray. There is a great coaching staff who work to teach the players our unique 'principles of play' and to teach them how to play in various shapes and formations to learn the game.

On top of that, we have our own school programme at Balerno High School, led by Paul Thomson, which provides the players with 18 hours of football per week. We have the best football science and medicine team in Scotland led by Mike Williams, sport psychology support, a bespoke education programme and a whole host of initiatives and staff to support the development and growth of our young players.

At the Academy, we also pride ourselves on the holistic development of the 'person' and not just the player. We create learning environments and give control to the players so that they make their own choices and

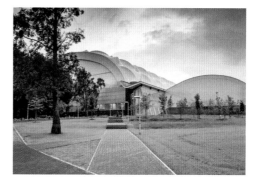

decisions, developing confidence and leadership skills, taking responsibility for themselves as they grow older and learning transferable skills that will see them into their adult life.

These are the three key areas that young players should consider, and parents should know that we take pride in excelling in them all.

Since 2014, what changes have you seen in the Academy?

In the past five years, the club has invested in the growth of the Academy year on year with a significant financial increase of over 40% since 2014. We are proud to have invested in:
• World class facilities for all teams at ORIAM
• Five Development Centres at U8 in Edinburgh, Fife, Forth Valley, West Lothian and Midlothian
• 15 full-time staff to drive progress in all Academy areas
    • A first-class Academy coaching staff, mentored by Darren Murray
        • Partnership with Balerno High School for 30 Hearts Academy players
        • The commitment to the development of a Hearts Women and Girls Academy
        • A full-time Under-18 squad

Will the Academy always play a vital role in the core identity of Hearts?

100%! A Hearts team should, and will, be full of young Academy graduates who will give the team energy, enthusiasm, intensity, coupled with fantastic skill and ability. A Hearts team will always have young players at the core of its identity!

Junior Jambos

HOW TO BECOME A JUNIOR JAMBO:

Junior Jambos is a membership dedicated to fans aged 12 years and under. It's a fantastic way to introduce youngsters to the club and inspire a life-long love of football, as well as enjoying exclusive events and giveaways.

For only £15, each member of Junior Jambos will receive the following:

- Membership package
- Membership certificate
- Membership Card
- Pin badge
- Pencil
- Sticker sheet
- £5 Clubstore voucher
- A personalised birthday and Christmas card from Jock the Jambo

EVENTS:

Members will be invited to three exclusive events throughout the 2019/20 season:

- November 2019: Training session at the Hearts Academy
- March 2020: Player Signing Session
- April 2020: Jock's Birthday Bash

Junior Jambos

GIVEAWAYS:

We'll be giving away a range of club experiences and merchandise to Junior Jambos members throughout the 2019/20 season, including:

- Tynecastle Park Stadium Tours
- Mascot experiences at every one of Hearts' Ladbrokes Premiership home fixtures
- Access to a first team training day at Tynecastle
- Free registration for a Hearts Community #PlaytheGame coaching course
- 2019/20 Home, Away and Third kits

CLUB BENEFITS:

Each Junior Jambos member will receive the following club benefits:

- 10% off non-sale items at the Hearts Clubstore when you show your membership card
- A Junior Jambos discount equivalent to an early bird discount on any HMFC Community Coaching Holiday Course

Sign up now at

heartsfc.co.uk

Thierry Henry

There were many great players gracing the turf that sunny afternoon at Murrayfield in July 2007. Xavi, Ronaldinho, Samuel Eto'o. But one of the best that day, and possibly ever, was Thierry Henry.

The match between Hearts and Barcelona - who disappointingly played in light blue rather than their traditional kit - finished 3-1 to the visitors but, for the fans who had come from all over, the score was unimportant. They were getting to watch their heroes - the best in the world.

Ronaldinho scored a penalty after Andrius Ksanavicius brought down Zambrotta in the box then Hearts' Finnish striker Juho Makela equalised just two minutes later, poking home from close range but the Jambos could not hold on until half-time.

Ronaldinho got his second of the day on 40 minutes, putting Barca ahead just before half-

time with a rare header. The King of Samba was then subbed off at half-time, watching the rest of the match from a fold-up chair next to the dug-out, wearing a fisherman's hat and his flip-flops.

Henry was not on the pitch in the first-half with Frank Rijkaard preferring Samuel Eto'o in attack – a tough headache to have - but Thierry was introduced at half-time, when the Dutchman brought seven players on.

Henry's impact was almost immediate as he helped kill the game off as a contest. The Frenchman made a brilliant run into the area before cutting back across goal to find young Giovani dos Santos who tapped into an open goal. In case you're wondering, Lionel Messi was rested after he had been on international duty.

It had been a surprise when Henry, at the age of

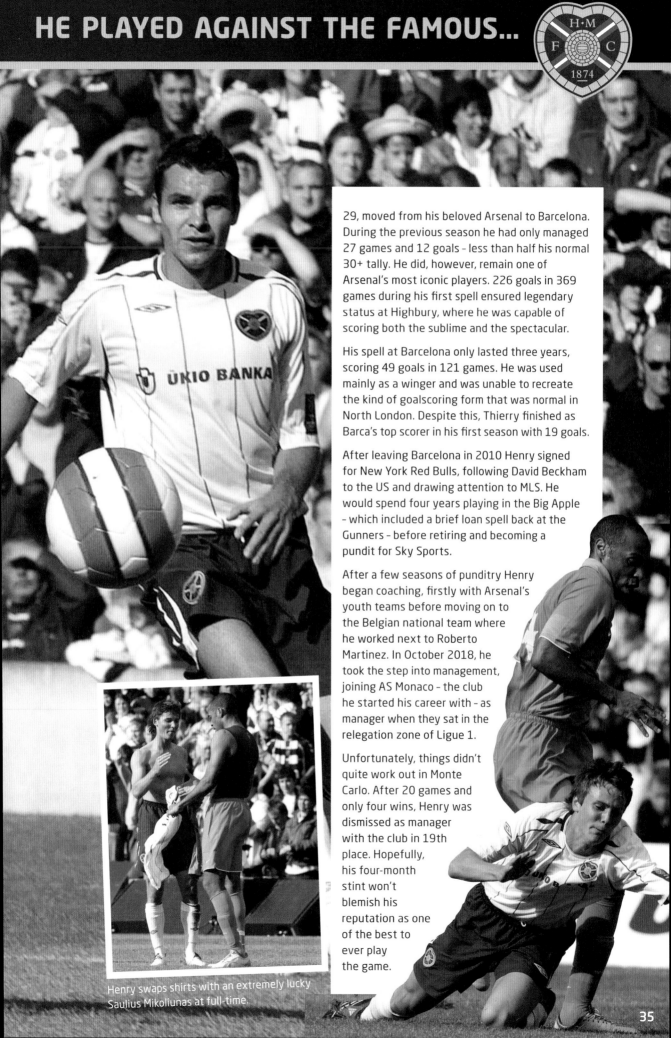

29, moved from his beloved Arsenal to Barcelona. During the previous season he had only managed 27 games and 12 goals - less than half his normal 30+ tally. He did, however, remain one of Arsenal's most iconic players. 226 goals in 369 games during his first spell ensured legendary status at Highbury, where he was capable of scoring both the sublime and the spectacular.

His spell at Barcelona only lasted three years, scoring 49 goals in 121 games. He was used mainly as a winger and was unable to recreate the kind of goalscoring form that was normal in North London. Despite this, Thierry finished as Barca's top scorer in his first season with 19 goals.

After leaving Barcelona in 2010 Henry signed for New York Red Bulls, following David Beckham to the US and drawing attention to MLS. He would spend four years playing in the Big Apple - which included a brief loan spell back at the Gunners - before retiring and becoming a pundit for Sky Sports.

After a few seasons of punditry Henry began coaching, firstly with Arsenal's youth teams before moving on to the Belgian national team where he worked next to Roberto Martinez. In October 2018, he took the step into management, joining AS Monaco - the club he started his career with - as manager when they sat in the relegation zone of Ligue 1.

Unfortunately, things didn't quite work out in Monte Carlo. After 20 games and only four wins, Henry was dismissed as manager with the club in 19th place. Hopefully, his four-month stint won't blemish his reputation as one of the best to ever play the game.

Henry swaps shirts with an extremely lucky Saulius Mikoliunas at full-time.

35

Gareth Southgate

The year was 2005. *You're Beautiful* by James Blunt was rising up the charts. England were a year away from a World Cup quarter-final defeat by Portugal, once again bowing out on penalties even though their Golden Generation was supposed to bring football home. Waistcoats were still untrendy.

The season that awaited Hearts was one of the most challenging in the club's history. Flying high at the top of the table after 10 games, manager George Burley was sacked. Valdas Ivanauskas eventually took over, getting the Jambos back on track as they achieved a second-placed finish for the first time in 14 years, as well as lifting the Scottish Cup at Hampden.

But the season only started when Gareth Southgate strode out onto the Tynecastle turf.

Middlesbrough paid a visit to the capital on a warm July evening that turned out to be relatively important in recent Gorgie times. Not because the future England manager was about to make his only ever appearance against Hearts – but because Rudi Skacel was about to make his debut in maroon.

The game itself finished 1-1. Yakubu put 'Boro ahead with a 77th-minute penalty before Andy Webster headed in from a corner to level five minutes later. The score-line wasn't too relevant, as friendly scores often aren't, but the team-sheets made for much more interesting reading.

Burley gave debuts to three new Czech signings: Roman Bednar, Michal Pospisil and Skacel. Edgaras Jankuaskas also made his first appearance, off the bench, during the second half.

Steve McClaren named a strong side – a side that would go on to finish as runners up in the UEFA Cup that year, losing 4-0 to Sevilla in the final. Five of the starting eleven against Hearts would start that final: Stuart Parnaby, Franck Queudrue, Southgate, Mark Viduka, and George Boateng. Another four would sit on the bench; Brad Jones, Ray Parlour, Ugo Ehiogu, and Yakubu.

When Southgate captained 'Boro against Hearts on that July night he was 34 years old, entering his final season as a player. In fact, eleven months later he would take over the helm at the Riverside as McClaren began his stint as England manager.

It was a little controversial as Southgate didn't have the required qualifications to manage a Premier League club but that was soon brushed aside as he guided 'Boro to 12th and 13th in his first two seasons as gaffer. However, in his third season they were relegated and in October 2009 he was sacked - despite being one point off the top of the Championship.

He went on to become the FA's head of elite development in January 2011 before being appointed the manager of England's U-21 team two years later. He spent three years in charge of the Young Lions which included a disappointing U-21 Euro Championship in 2015 where they finished last in their group.

However, when Sam Allardyce resigned after one game in charge of the Three Lions, Southgate stepped in as caretaker after winning 82% of his games as U-21 boss. Two months later, in November 2016, he was awarded the job permanently.

As England boss his win percentage sits at only 58% but he has been widely regarded as a huge success. This is largely because of England's performance in Russia over the summer, where they eventually finished fourth after losing to Croatia in the semi-finals.

On paper it was an impressive feat, but it was made better by the fact his squad was not expected to achieve much. When England eventually flew home, they were even disappointed that they had not made it to the final. A narrow win over Tunisia, a hammering of Panama, a penalty win over Colombia and a stress-free quarter-final over Sweden. Hardly the worst opposition, but they survived banana skins that the Golden Generation may have slipped on.

The job was originally considered by many as a poisoned chalice but the 57-times capped defender managed to get the media on-board, created a likeable squad and introduced a harmony into the team which ensured England's best finish at a World Cup since Italia '90.

Kevin Keegan

Keegan lines up for England against Scotland at Hampden in 1982.

Tuesday, May 25th 1984 was supposed to be all about Hearts legend Alex MacDonald but there was one man in maroon who the crowd were distracted by.

17,853 lucky fans got to see Kevin Keegan pull on the famous maroon jersey as part of McDonald's testimonial against Rangers at Tynecastle Park. They weren't let down either as Keegan took time to sign autographs ahead of the match before putting on a fantastic performance, full of flair, as the game finished 3-2 to Rangers.

Keegan, 33 at that point, managed 73 minutes and got an assist, linking up with Hearts hero John Robertson for a superb goal. The then-England captain, who had just achieved promotion with Newcastle United before his retirement, played superbly in the midfield alongside player-manager Alex MacDonald, and up-and-coming midfielder Gary Mackay and linked up well.

Mighty Mouse certainly didn't disappoint, with flicks and tricks mesmerising the Rangers players and inspiring the Hearts players to put on a show of their own. However, it was not the last time he would play at Tynecastle.

Monday 27th July 1992 was another testimonial date, this time for Robbo. By this point Keegan was 41 and had been officially retired for eight years. Now he was back as Newcastle manager but that would not stop him playing.

The game was watched by 11,000 fans at Tynecastle and they saw

Hearts beat a Newcastle side that would achieve promotion to the Premier League at the end of the season. Ian Baird scored just minutes into the second-half and there was no further action as Hearts ran out 1-0 winners.

This time, Keegan only managed 20 minutes – but it didn't matter to the fans who had come to watch, they had still seen one of the best.

The striker started his career as a 17-year-old at Fourth Divison side Scunthorpe United before joining Liverpool in 1971. He would soon become a legend at Anfield, winning the division title and UEFA Cup in only his second season.

Overall, his time on Merseyside was an enormous success. He picked up three first division titles, an FA Cup, two UEFA Cups and the European Cup in 1977 – in his last game for the club. Keegan had announced his intention to leave Liverpool and play abroad, so after 323 appearances and 100 goals, he joined Hamburg in the German Bundesliga for £500,000.

In his first season he was awarded France Football's European Footballer of the Year award – or as it is now known, the Ballon d'Or and he won it again the following year, as well as winning the Bundesliga title.

In 1980 Keegan joined Southampton – a shock transfer at the time – and despite two good seasons on the south coast he would join Newcastle United, who were still in the Second Division.

He was an immediate hit on Tyneside, scoring 48 goals in 78 games. His form helped get them promoted and he became a hero, alongside Peter Beardsley and Chris Waddle. He would retire at the end of the 1984 season, leaving the pitch in a helicopter in his final game, still dressed in his kit.

He would go on to become one of the best managers in Newcastle United's history, as well as getting Fulham and Manchester City promoted to the Championship and Premiership. In between those two jobs he also took charge of England during Euro 2000.

WHERE'S JOCK?

JOCK THE JAMBO WAS CHEERING FOR HEARTS DURING THE SCOTTISH CUP FINAL LAST SEASON, BUT CAN YOU SPOT WHERE HE IS?

Answers on page 60-61.

BORN:
29th MAY 1995

Craig started at Rosebank United but signed for Rangers at 15, initially playing as a striker.

He won the Youth Cup in 2014 – beating Hearts on penalties in the final. Craig scored the equaliser in the 90th minute with a header from the edge of the box, but he was released in January 2016 after loan spells at Berwick Rangers and Clyde.

He quickly joined Livingston, but he did think about quitting the full-time game. After getting four Highers at secondary school, Craig thought about a job outside of football or enrolling at university.

Three months after being released by Rangers, he scored a headed winner for Livingston to beat Mark Warburton's side 1-0 at the Tony Macaroni Arena.

Livingston were relegated but, with Craig as captain, they bounced back to the Championship before gaining promotion to the Premiership the next again year.

In Craig's first year in top flight football, he was named in the PFA Team of the Year.

Craig has represented Scotland once, at Under-19 level, in 2014. He played 149 times for Livingston, scoring 18 goals.

CRAIG HALKETT

New Kit 2019/20

Michael Smith, **Steven MacLean** and **Peter Haring** share a laugh.

John Souttar tries his best blue steel.

What are you hiding there, **Bozzie**?

Hearts Women's player and Jambos fan **Claire Delworth** poses in the new Umbro home shirt.

Uche Ikpeazu cracks a smile.

Emily Mutch and **Bobby Zlamal** discuss the GK Union.

Have you got this in a small?

45

PLAYER OF THE YEAR *Awards*

STEVEN NAISMITH PICKED UP TWO PLAYER OF THE YEAR GONGS IN THE GORGIE SUITE AT HEARTS' ANNUAL AWARDS CEREMONY IN MAY 2019, SPONSORED BY MERCEDES-BENZ OF EDINBURGH.

On-loan Norwich striker **Naismith** won both **Fans' Player** and **Players' Player of the Year** after a season in which he scored 14 goals in 27 appearances.

He wasn't the only one to pick up awards as eight other prizes were dished out.

The Youth awards were the first to be announced with Scottish Cup Final-starter **Aaron Hickey** picking up the **Youth to Pro** award, recognising Aaron's adjustment to life as a full-time professional.

Next up was the **Reserves Player of the Year**, voted for by the coaches. That went to Bulgarian centre-half **Alex Petkov**, who was also included in the Scottish Cup Final squad after a fantastic 2018-19 season.

The **Overall Young Player of the Year** was awarded to **John Souttar**, who won it for the

PLAYER OF THE YEAR
Awards

second year in a row, 22-year-old John enjoyed a fantastic twelve months that saw him captain his club - with one of the best records ever - and pick up his first three caps for Scotland.

The **Doc Melvin Award** was next to be presented and it went to club historians **Bill Smith** and **David Speed**.

After a short dinner break, Craig Levein was on hand to present the **Special Recognition Prize**, which was won by a speechless **Andy Kirk**, head coach of the Reserves side. Andy enjoyed a fantastic first full-year in the role, which culminated in lifting the Reserve League Cup in April.

Save of the Season was the next award, fiercely contested by the two first-team goalkeepers **Bobby Zlamal** and Colin Doyle. This time, Bobby was the winner after his fantastic - and crucial - Scottish Cup semi-final save against Inverness when he tipped Joe Chalmers' free-kick onto the crossbar.

Steven Naismith then picked up his first award, the **Fans' Player of the Year**. Despite injuries last season Naisy still had a huge impact on and off the field, playing his way into the hearts of fans around Gorgie.

There were then the awards for **Goal of the Season** and **Memorable Moment** - which both occurred on one cold December night in the green half of Edinburgh.

Olly Lee's rocket to beat fierce rivals Hibs 1-0 was the obvious **Goal of the Season** winner, and that night in general won **Memorable Moment**, for which **Michael Smith** picked up the gong.

Finally, it was time for the big award - **Players' Player of the Year**. There were votes for Bobby Zlamal, Arnaud Djoum and Michael Smith, but the overall winner was once again **Steven Naismith**, picking up his second award of the night.

BIG TYN

How well do you know your Jambos?

01 How many goals did Uche Ikpeazu score last season?
_____

02 What number does Christophe Berra wear?
_____

03 Who did John Souttar make his Scotland debut against?
_____

04 What country does Bobby Burns play for?
_____

05 Who is known as the Queen of Hearts?

06 True or False? Raheem Sterling and Jordan Henderson have played against Hearts.
_____

07 True or False? Andy Kirk used to play for Hearts.
_____

08 Who did Connor Smith make his debut again?
_____

09 Which club did Hearts sign Jamie Walker from?
_____

10 How many goals did Peter Haring score in the 18/19 season?

50

IE QUIZ ??

Put your Hearts knowledge to the test!

11 What date did Hearts beat Hibs 5-1 in the Scottish Cup final?

_____

12 Who scored Hearts' first goal of 2019?

_____

13 Who made the most appearances in the entire 2018/19 season?

_____

14 Who is younger – Harry Cochrane or Anthony McDonald?

_____

15 Who was Hearts manager when the Jambos won the Scottish Cup in 1998?

_____

16 What number does Craig Halkett wear?

_____

17 Who made more appearances in the league last season - Callumn Morrison or Uche Ikpeazu?

18 Who is known as The Jambo Soldier?

_____

19 How old was Steven MacLean at the start of the 19/20 season?

_____

20 Who scored Hearts' goal in the 2019 Scottish Cup Final?

Answers on page 60-61.

10

17

08

51

HALL of FAME

THE 1998 SCOTTISH CUP WINNING TEAM WERE AMONG THE CLUB LEGENDS INDUCTED INTO THE HEART OF MIDLOTHIAN HALL OF FAME LAST NOVEMBER.

A sold-out Gorgie Suite welcomed Hearts heroes from the distant and not-so-distant past for a night of nostalgia at Tynecastle Park.

Walter Kidd joined host Peter Martin on stage as the former Hearts captain became the first inductee of the night. With 462 competitive appearances to his name, 'Zico' received a hero's welcome from the capacity crowd.

Next up was another club stalwart in the shape of **Alan Anderson**. A key defensive figure during the 1960s, Alan amassed an impressive 475 appearances for the boys in maroon - scoring 31 goals.

Jock White was next to etch his name into the Hall of Fame. Described by Club Historian David Speed as being "the Rudi Skacel of his day", Jock scored an incredible 183 goals in 312 competitive appearances during the 1920s.

Hearts legend John Robertson described him as one of Hearts finest ever strikers and the club was honoured to welcome his grandson on to the stage to accept the award on the late Jock's behalf.

HALL of FAME

Speaker Eric Milligan took to the stage to share his Hearts memories before the Wallace Mercer Special Recognition Award was given to the late **Pilmar Smith**, who sadly passed away earlier that month. Craig Levein accepted the award on his behalf and spoke warmly of the man whom he described as a very close friend.

Drew Busby then became the fourth inductee of the night. Drew scored 84 goals in 256 competitive Hearts appearances and received a rapturous ovation from the crowd and spoke fondly of his time at the club.

HALL of FAME

Finally, the stage was set for the **1998 Scottish Cup team**. The likes of Thomas Flogel, Gary Locke, Neil McCann, Colin Cameron and Dave McPherson were all in attendance, as were the management duo Jim Jefferies and Billy Brown. 'When the Hearts went on to win the Scottish Cup, we were there' rang out around the Gorgie Suite as the night drew to a close in spectacular fashion.

THE 200 CLUB

Over the course of the last 12 months, we've been carefully compiling fact files on all 73 players who have pulled on the maroon jersey more than 200 times. Some names might be totally new to you (ask your grandad about them!) and some might be instantly recognisable! So, we present to you a select few of those lucky players...

No. 19: Tommy Walker

"Arguably Hearts' finest ever footballer, but unquestionably its greatest sportsman and ambassador."

When he was the Hearts manager, Tommy Walker was the architect of the superb teams that won every domestic trophy and played in European competition for the first time. Tommy also enjoyed a distinguished playing career with Hearts. His passing, dribbling and shooting skills were universally acclaimed, as was his sportsmanship.

He was born in Livingston in May 1915 and after signing for Hearts he wrote to the manager, Willie McCartney, to say how grateful he was.

In a short period of time, Tommy also revealed class on the field, with his brilliant ball control and skill in possession. Tommy was on the path to become

Britain's finest playmaker.

He made a scoring debut against Hibernian in August 1932 and, within months, Hearts had English clubs chasing his transfer.

In 1934, when he was only 19, Tommy earned the first of 20 consecutive International caps.

Standing almost 5'9" and weighing just over eleven stone, he was quick and alert around the penalty box and Hearts' supporters relished his creative style and powerful shot.

He also played against SK Rapid in August 1934 when the Austrian side became the first overseas club to appear in Gorgie.

After leaving for Chelsea years before, he returned in December 1948, as assistant manager to Davie McLean. Tommy hung up his boots, after scoring a remarkable 224 goals for Hearts in 408 competitive appearances.

Tommy took over team affairs in 1951 and fashioned brilliantly balanced squads that led Hearts through its finest era. In record-breaking style, his teams won the League Championship twice; the Scottish Cup once; and the Scottish League Cup four times. As well as that, Tommy introduced European football to Tynecastle for the first time.

In November 1960, Tommy received an OBE from Her Majesty the Queen for his services to football.

He left Hearts in 1966 but returned again in 1974 to serve on the board as a director. He retired in 1980 and it was a sad day in Edinburgh when he passed away in 1993.

Tommy was the dictionary definition of a Hearts legend, and a name that any young Hearts fan should know.

After all, most youngsters will know his great-nephew Jamie Walker, who returned to Hearts in the summer of 2019. The family name continues.

No. 47: *Jim Jefferies*

Born in November 1950 in Musselburgh, Jim made 310 competitive appearances and scored six goals before moving to Berwick Rangers in November 1981. He played in the Scottish Cup Final in 1976 and captained the squad that won the First Division Championship in 1979/80. The epitome of a great servant both on and off the field, the crowning achievement of Jim's two spells as manager was Hearts' victory in the Scottish Cup Final in 1998. A Hearts man through-and-through.

No. 54: *Gary Mackay*

Born in Edinburgh in January 1964, Gary is very much a local hero who gave Hearts over 16 years of dedicated playing service. After signing from Salvesen Boys Club in July 1980, he smashed all the appearance records with 737 for the club, including a record 515 league matches. His midfield graft and skill brought out the best in his colleagues and Gary helped Hearts to achieve runners-up position in the league on three occasions. He also played in two Scottish Cup finals and one League Cup final. Gary earned four international caps and when he kissed the Hearts badge, he meant it.

No. 55: *John Robertson*

Born in Edinburgh in October 1964, John is possibly the greatest scorer in Hearts history, breaking a number of established records after he was signed from Edina Hibs Boys Club in January 1981. "Robbo" made his debut in February 1982 and after he started scoring, he never stopped, eventually hitting 310 in 720 matches for the club - his total is second only to Willie Bauld. Three times his goals inspired Hearts to runners-up position in the League and the international striker also took part in two Scottish Cup finals and one League Cup final. In addition, he hit 27 goals against Hibs which is unsurpassed in the history of Edinburgh football, earning him the nickname "The Hammer of Hibs". John finally earned a winners' medal when he was on the bench (sadly unused) in the 1998 Scottish Cup final. He was head coach of Hearts from November 2004 to May 2005.

No. 59: *Craig Levein*

Born in Aberdour in October 1964, Craig was the classiest defender Hearts ever had and the Fifer would have become the finest sweeper in Britain had he not suffered a series of knee injuries, which forced him to retire in 1997. Craig was a star man as Hearts came so close to a League and Cup double in 1985/86. He was also an established internationalist and played at the 1990 World Cup. After 401 competitive games during which he scored 17 goals, Craig moved into management and is now in his second spell in charge of the club. He has also played a key role in restructuring the club after administration.

No. 63: *John Colquhoun*

Born in July 1963 in Stirling, John went on to score 82 goals in 424 competitive matches. He started with Stirling Albion but moved to Celtic as a youngster. However, it didn't work out at Parkhead and he joined Hearts in 1985. He scored on his debut for the Jambos against former club Celtic, and it was the start of an instantly successful Tynecastle career. Essentially a creative winger, John had a huge range of attacking skills and when he was in the team Hearts always had a chance of winning. He was inspirational during Hearts' vain bid to win the double in '86 and fully merited his inclusion in the national team.

No. 66: *Dave McPherson*

In every sense of the word, Dave was a giant in the centre of Hearts' defence, making 364 competitive appearances and scoring 32 goals during two spells in maroon. Dave signed for the Jambos from Rangers in 1987 and within two years was playing in the national team after being named Hearts' club captain. After some near-misses in terms of winning honours, Dave was a key man in the '98 Scottish Cup final win. He was a familiar face on the plane for Craig Levein when they flew to Italy for the 1990 World Cup.

ANSWERS

SPOT THE BALL (PAGE 22)

BIG TYNIE QUIZ (PAGE 50-51)

01	Eight	11	19th May 2012
02	Six	12	Sean Clare
03	Belgium	13	Olly Lee - 41
04	Northern Ireland	14	Harry Cochrane
05	Ann Budge	15	Jim Jefferies
06	True	16	26
07	True	17	Callumn Morrison
08	Kilmarnock	18	Clevid Dikamona
09	Wigan Athletic	19	36
10	Seven	20	Ryan Edwards

JAMBO WORDSEARCH (PAGE 23)

D	L	E	I	F	T	A	E	H	W	H
N	D	N	R	Z	L	H	H	K	R	D
F	A	E	R	K	H	D	L	E	O	T
R	Y	I	Y	U	M	T	K	Y	Y	D
K	C	G	S	M	B	L	L	E	C	E
K	C	R	R	M	A	E	K	N	K	L
Y	E	O	K	W	I	C	S	C	M	W
K	H	G	J	M	I	T	M	O	Q	O
V	C	R	K	H	P	H	H	M	R	R
F	U	J	S	K	A	C	E	L	B	T
W	H	A	L	K	E	T	T	R	M	H

WHERE'S JOCK? (PAGE 40-41)

61

Behind the Scenes
at Tynecastle